SCIENCE ENCYCLOPEDIA

FORCE, ELECTRICITY,
METALS AND NON-METALS

An imprint of Om Books International

Contents

FORCE

Force is described by intuitive concepts, such as a push or pull. In physics, a force is any interaction that tends to change the motion of objects. In contrast, a force may cause the object with a certain mass to change its velocity (which involves moving the object from the state of rest). Since force exhibits both magnitude as well as direction, it is a vector quantity.

Force is measured in the SI unit of Newton and represented by the symbol F. Force helps objects to slow down or accelerate. Ice-skating, skydiving or any other physical activity, all use force.

Besides a simple push or pull, force also has further applications. Force can be of different types, magnitude or direction. In physics, force refers to the interaction between two objects to change the motion of an object.

Turning Forces

The turning effect by a force around a fixed point or pivot is called a moment. For example, this could be a door opening around a fixed hinge or a spanner turning around a fixed nut. The size of a movement depends on two factors: the size of the force applied and the perpendicular distance from the pivot to the line of action of the force.

Force requirement

Why is less force used to open a door when we push it at the side furthest from the hinge rather than at the side closest to the hinge? Pushing a door open closer to the hinge requires more force to be exerted because the distance of the force from the hinge is smaller.

Now consider opening the door by pushing towards the outside of the door, the point furthest away from the hinge. It requires lesser force because the distance of the point of force applied is further away from the pivot point, that is the hinge.

When a body under the influence of a net external force is rotated about a pivot, the body tends to move in the direction in which the force is applied. Examples of the turning effect of force are the force applied to a door knob that makes it open on its hinge and a driver steering the wheel by applying a force on its rim.

Balancing moments

When an object is not turning around a pivot, the total clockwise moment should be exactly balanced by the total anti-clockwise moment. It is said that the opposing moments are balanced, where the sum of the clockwise moments equals to the sum of the anti-clockwise moments. Let us take the example of a see-saw. It has a pivot in the middle. The person on the right exerts a force downward that causes a clockwise moment. The person on the left exerts a force downward that causes an anti-clockwise moment. If both the people have similar weights and sit at equal distances from the pivot, then the see-saw will balance. This is because the total clockwise moment is balanced by the total anti-clockwise moment.

However, the see-saw can still balance if the people weigh differently. To do this, the person who weighs more must sit closer to the pivot. This reduces the size of the moment, so the opposing moments get balanced again.

A see-saw can still balance if the people weigh differently.

Stretch and Pull

Elasticity is the ability of a distorted material body to return to its original shape and size when the forces causing the distortion are eliminated. A body with this ability is said to perform elastically. The force you use to stretch an elastic body is the same with which the body snaps back to its original size. That's why a rubber band hurts!

Elastic limit

Many solid materials exhibit elastic behaviour; however, there is a limit to the amount of force and distortion till which the elastic recovery is possible for any given material. Elastic limit is the maximum stress or force per unit area that a solid object can withstand before the start of permanent distortion. Beyond this limit, stress causes a material to yield or flow. The elastic limit denotes the end of elastic behaviour for these objects and the beginning of plastic behaviour. For most fragile materials, stress beyond the elastic limit results in a fracture. If you consider different types of rubbers, some rubbers have a high elastic limit; for example, a balloon. You can blow it up to a certain extent and yet, it will retain its original shape when deflated. However, consider a rubber band. If you try to stretch it to the size of a balloon, it may snap. This is because its elastic limit is lower than that of a balloon.

Girl doing elastic rope exercise.

Variation in elastic limit

The elastic limit varies from object to object. Some forms of rubber can be stretched up to 1,000 per cent of their original size. In contrast, a steel wire can be stretched by only about 1 per cent of its original length. This is because their structures are different and the tensile force required for elastic extension in rubber is less than that required for steel.

The molecules in a piece of elastic are coiled. When the elastic is pulled, the molecules uncoil and the elastic stretches. When released, the molecules coil again and the elastic comes back to its original shape.

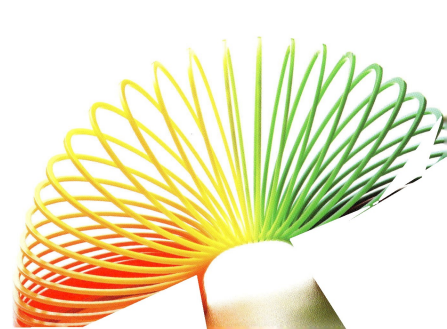

Types of Forces

In science, force is not limited to only one definition, but is generally defined as something that causes the motion of an object. There can be two cases on the application of force. One case can be when force is applied to a stationary body; it sets the stationary body in motion in the direction of the force applied. In the second case, the body could be moving with uniform velocity and with the application of force, it gets accelerated in the same direction as earlier.

Types of forces

An object is simultaneously affected by different types of physical forces like thrust, drag and torque. Force can fundamentally be of three types; nuclear, electromagnetic and gravitational. As a consequence of these forces, some other forces are generated, which are called non-fundamental forces. These include normal force, friction, tension, elastic force, fictitious force, torque and applied force, among others. Applied force is the force applied to an object or body, where a frictional force is used to stop a body in motion.

Calculating force

The interaction between two objects to change the motion of an object is called force. As this interaction stops, there remains no force. Sir Isaac Newton, with his laws of motion, and Einstein, with his theory of relativity, made the concept of force clear. Force can be calculated by,

$$F = m \times a$$

where, m = mass of the object, which is considered constant and a = acceleration.

FUN FACT

The unit of measure for force is newton (N). This is indeed named after Sir Isaac Newton, who laid down the Newton's laws of motion.

Monorail works on electromagnetic force.

Tension

When we stretch an object, a force called tension is generated as in a spring; it is the opposite of compression. In physics, the best example is that of the tension in a rope and pulley system. This is a force that is transmitted along a string, wire, rope or cable that is imagined as a weightless, frictionless object that cannot be broken or stretched when it is pulled tightly by the forces at opposite ends.

Importance of tension

Similar to all forces, tension can hasten objects or cause them to bend. Being able to calculate tension is an important skill for physics students, as well as for engineers and architects. They need to know if the tension on a given rope or cable can withstand the strain caused by the weight of the object before yielding and breaking in order to construct safe and strong buildings.

Uses of tension

This can be better understood by simply taking the example of an object being pulled by a rope. We do not apply force on an object directly, but it is applied through the rope. Here, the object being pulled also exerts an equal and opposite force. The magnitude of the force remains directly proportional to the tension magnitude. If objects are placed at both ends, there are two possibilities. Either the acceleration is zero and the system is at equilibrium, or there is some force and acceleration.

Tension is created in the rope when playing tug of war.

Weightlifter

Is it a force?

It is debatable whether tension is a type of force, but it has the SI unit of Newton. "Tension" as a force has many applications in our day-to-day life. Even in biological science, it has many uses, such as:

1. Cell membrane tension causes changes in the cell shape and its motility.

2. Tension in the land causes rocks to break down.

3. In DNA, it is found that tension stabilises the chromosomes.

4. Tension works in the body of a weightlifter while practising with weights.

Torsion

Torsion is a type of force that can be called as the twisting of an object. It can be defined as a moment applied along the longitudinal axis of any object. On the upper and lower parts of an object, force is applied equally in opposite directions. It is measured in Newton metres (N.m) or foot-pound force (ft.lbf).

Rear wheels of a car.

Applications of torsion

Torsion has many important applications. Some of them are as follows:

1. Shafts loaded with torsion have application in engineering. It is used in the rear wheels of automobiles and in almost all rotating machineries.

2. It comes to use when we tighten a nut using a wrench.

3. It is also useful for opening the cap of a bottle.

4. A wide variety of torsion springs are used for door handles and clipboards.

5. The concept of torsion is applied in running shoes to avoid the chances of foot injuries for runners.

Effects of torsion

The effects of a torsional load applied to a bar are given as follows:

1. To impart an angular displacement of one end of a cross-section with respect to the other.

2. To setup shear stresses on any cross-section of the bar perpendicular to its axis.

FUN FACT

A catapult works because of the force of torsion. A rubber band and paper clip act as a simplification of the process. When the band is pulled back, torsion propels the clip into motion.

Unscrewing a bottle cap is an example of torsion.

Running shoes work on the basis of torsion.

Torque

Torque refers to the measure of how much a force acting on an object causes that object to rotate. The object rotates about its axis, which is called the pivot point "O". The force is denoted as "F". The distance between the pivot point and the point where the force acts is termed as the moment arm, it is denoted by "r". Note that this distance, r, is also a vector and points from the axis of the rotation to the point where the force acts.

How it works?

Consider a heavy box on the ground that you want to turn. You can either push it or take a wrench and try to turn the box. It depends on the length of the wrench and the force required to turn that box. The longer the wrench, the lesser the force that will be required. This force is called torque. It can be defined as a force used to rotate or turn things. Torque is the product of the lever arm distance and the force applied. The symbol of torque is τ. Torque depends on the force applied, the length of the lever arm and the angle between the force applied and the lever arm. The length of the lever arm is an important factor. Choosing it appropriately can greatly reduce the amount of force that is applied. The unit of torque is Newton Metre (N•m). A crowbar, used to open jammed doors or boxes that have been nailed shut, works on the principles of torque.

Application of torque

There are many applications where torque is very important, some are given as follows:

1. Levers, pulleys, gears and other simple machines.
2. Automobiles.
3. Hand pumps and doors.

Torque force is applied to change the tyre with a wheel wrench.

Stress

Stress is the physical quantity used to express the internal forces that the neighbouring particles of any continuous material exert on each other. Stress and strain are very closely related. Strain is the result of stress and any internal movement because of stress is strain.

How is it expressed?

Mathematically, stress is measured as the force per unit area. Thus, the unit of stress becomes Newton per square metre, which is also called a pascal. The area that is used in stress is the cross-sectional area. Strain on the other hand is the change in the length of a certain continuous material divided by the original length. So, strain has no unit and is simply the ratio. Therefore, if you stretch a rubber band, you can easily calculate the strain on it by comparing its initial length with the change in its length.

Importance of stress

Stress and strain are very important for measuring the elasticity of a material. The stress versus strain graph tells us if a material is brittle, ductile or elastic. The very fundamental law that relates stress and strain is called the Hooke's law. Hooke's law states that stress is directly proportional to the strain. The slope of the linear region, that is, the constant for the proportionality is known as Young's modulus.

Stress force in pole vault.

Different material strength

A ductile material fails at a much higher strain as compared to a brittle material. The area under the curve is called the toughness of the material, which is basically a measure of the ability of the material to absorb energy before breaking when external stress is applied. Thus, the toughness of the ductile material is much higher than that of the brittle material.

Pressure

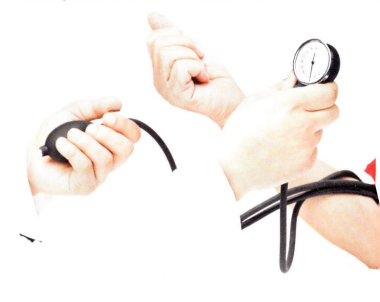

Pressure is a physical quantity derived from force and area. Pressure is normally expressed as the force exerted per unit area. This means that the force or the component of force that is applied perpendicularly to a certain area is the force in that area. Force is measured in Newton and the area in meter square. Thus, the pressure becomes Newton per metre square.

How it works?

The unit of pressure is called pascal. Pressure is also measured in relation to the atmospheric pressure. The other commonly used unit of pressure is Psi, which refers to pound per square inch. Pressure is also measured in nanometric units.

The more the weight, the higher the pressure.

Exact and opposite reaction

Pressure is highly dependent on area. For example, if you push your thumb against the wall, the wall will not be damaged. However, if you push a board pin with the same amount of force, it might penetrate the wall. Pressure acts equally on all surfaces. It comes from Newton's third law of motion. Hence, when you are pushing that pin into the wall, the pin is also exerting pressure on your finger. However, because the head of the pin has a larger area, the same force gets distributed over a larger area and thereby does not hurt your finger.

Water pressure used for cleaning.

Momentum

Momentum is the result of the second law of motion as proposed by Newton. The second law of motion states that the vector sum of all the forces acting on an object is equal to the mass multiplied by the acceleration of that object. In other words, we get the definition of force from this law. The force acting on an object for a certain time gives us the momentum. Or, momentum is force multiplied by time.

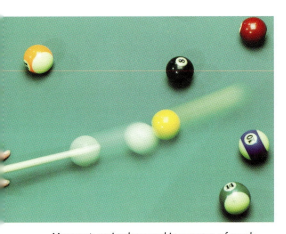

Momentum is observed in a game of pool; that is, if one ball stops dead after the collision, the other ball will continue away with all the momentum.

It is a vector

Momentum is a vector quantity; it is conserved and dependent upon a reference frame. First, it is a vector as force is a vector quantity. Rather, velocity is a vector and momentum is mass times velocity. Next, momentum is conserved. This means that the net change in the momentum of a closed system is always zero. Again, momentum is dependent on a reference frame because velocity is dependent on a reference frame.

Measure of motion

Momentum is also said to be the measure of motion. It is a very casual definition. This explains why a truck and bicycle, both travelling at the same speed, have different stopping distances. The truck goes on for a long distance before coming to a halt, whereas a bicycle will stop within just a few feet. The matter of fact is that a huge truck, even if it moves at a very low speed, has a very high momentum as compared to a small car with very high speed, simply because the truck is very heavy and has a higher mass.

Conservation of momentum

The momentum of any collection of objects is equal to the vector sum of the momentum of the individual objects. In accordance with Newton's third law of motion, these particles apply equal and opposite forces on each other, so any variation in the momentum of one particle is exactly adjusted by an equal and opposite variation in the momentum of another particle. Thus, when there is no net external force acting on a collection of particles, there is never a change in their total momentum, which is what the law of conservation of momentum states.

Newton's cradle displays how the momentum from one object can move to another.

Electromagnetic Forces

Electromagnetism is the study of the electromagnetic force, that is, a type of physical interaction, that occurs between electrically charged particles. The force experienced due to the electromagnetic fields, like electric or magnetic, is called electromagnetic force. It is one of the four fundamental interactions that exist in nature. Strong, weak and gravitational are the other interactions.

Infinite range

Electromagnetic force is the force exerted by the electromagnetic interaction of electrically charged or magnetically polarised particles or bodies. It is one of the four fundamental forces, and manifests itself through the forces between the charges (Coulomb's law) and the magnetic force. These forces are described through the Lorentz force law. Theoretically, both magnetic and electric forces are manifestations of an exchange force that involves the exchange of photons. Electromagnetic force has an infinite range, which obeys the conventional, inverse-square law.

An electromagnetic crane used in a metal scrap yard.

Electromagnetic induction

Electromagnetism is a manifestation of both electricity and magnetism. Both fields are different aspects of electromagnetism and hence are intrinsically related. Therefore, an altering electric field creates a magnetic field; conversely, an altering magnetic field creates an electric field. The effect is known as electromagnetic induction. This principle is the basis of the operation of electrical generators, motors and transformers. Magnetic and electric fields are convertible with relative motion. In quantum electrodynamics, electromagnetic interactions between charged particles can be calculated using the method of Feynman diagrams.

Centrifugal Force

Centrifugal force is an outward force that draws a rotating body away from the axis of rotation. This force is mainly caused by the inertia of the object. In physics, centrifugal force is the tendency of an object that follows a curved path to fly away from the centre of curvature. It is basically not a true force but a form of inertia.

A centrifuge rapidly rotates containers to apply centrifugal force to its contents.

Force for convenience

This force is described or grouped as a force of convenience because it balances the centripetal force that is described as a true force. If a ball is swung at the end of a rope, the rope exerts a centripetal force on the ball and causes it to follow a curved path. During the rotation, the ball exerts centrifugal force on the rope, which tends to break the rope and fly off on a tangent path. The effects of centrifugal force can be controlled and even harnessed for various useful applications. This force is applied in centrifuges and engine governors. Highway curves are tilted to prevent the centrifugal force from forcing the cars outwards off the road.

Increasing the force

Centrifugal force can be increased by increasing either the speed of rotation, mass of the body or radius, that is, distance of the body from the centre of the curve. Increasing either mass or radius will increase the centrifugal force equivalently, but increasing the speed of rotation will increase it in proportion to the square of speed. For instance, a 10 times increase in speed, say from 10 to 100 revolutions per minute, will increase the centrifugal force by a factor of 100. This force is expressed as a multiple of "g", the symbol for normal gravitational force.

Formula and units

Centrifugal force if measured in pounds can be calculated by the formula wv2/gr, where "w" stands for the weight of the object in pounds, and "v" represents the velocity in feet per second. The acceleration of gravity (32 feet per second) is "g". "r" is the radius of the circle in feet. There are many instances where centrifugal force is necessary. Children love to see the juggler's tricks in the circus. These could only be possible because of the existence of centrifugal force. In the dairy industry, cream is extracted from milk on the basis of centrifugal action. Besides these, there are numerous examples where centrifugal action is used for a beneficial reason in life.

Centripetal Force

Centripetal force is a force that allows a body to keep moving in a curved path. Its direction is always at a right angle to the velocity of the body and towards the fixed point of the instantaneous centre of curvature of the path. Any motion in a curved path represents accelerated motion, which needs a force that should be directed towards the centre of the curvature. This force associated with it is known as the centripetal force, meaning "centre-seeking" force.

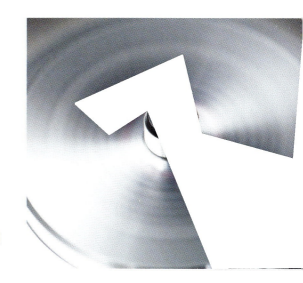

Acceleration

An object moving in a circle experiences acceleration. Even if the object is moving along the perimeter of a circle with a fixed speed, the velocity still changes and subsequently, the object attains acceleration. The direction of this acceleration is towards the centre of the circle. In accordance with Newton's second law, any object that experiences acceleration must also experience a force in the same direction as the direction of the acceleration. Thus, for an object moving in a circle, there must be an inward force acting upon it in order to cause its inward acceleration. This is sometimes referred to as the centripetal force requirement.

A Ferris wheel uses centripetal force.

How is it expressed?

The effective centripetal force on any object having a mass "m" moving at a tangential speed "v" along a path with the radius of curvature "r" is given as:

$F = mv^2/r$

Without a net centripetal force, no object can travel in a circular motion. In reality, if all the applied forces are balanced, then the object in motion continues in a straight line at a fixed constant speed.

Factors affecting centripetal force

The centripetal force required to keep an object moving in a circle increases if:

- the mass of the object increases
- the speed of the object increases
- the radius of the circle in which it is travelling decreases

Equilibrium of Forces

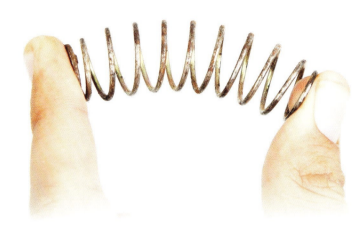

To consider a rigid body with its momentum in a conserved state, having attained equilibrium, we can take the example of a spring being compressed and the spring resisting the compression. Soon, any further pressure exerted is met with an equal resistive force from the spring so that it cannot be compressed further. This is called mechanical equilibrium. Equilibrium can be dynamic or static, depending on whether the object is in motion or at rest.

Dynamic equilibrium

Dynamic equilibrium is a condition, where in a reversible process, the reaction is proceeding at an equal rate in both forward and backward directions, and the net change in the reaction is zero. In simple words, it refers to a state of balance that is achieved by two forces in motion. We can take the example of the opening of a soda bottle or the dissociation of acetic acid. If we open a soda bottle and take out half of the liquid, then, after some time, equilibrium is attained as some molecules of carbon dioxide go from liquid to gaseous state and an equal amount of molecules transform from gaseous to liquid phase. Both reactions occur at the same rate and the state of equilibrium is attained.

Dynamic equilibrium.

Static equilibrium

Static equilibrium is a condition where a body is static; force will have to be applied in order to move the object. For an object to be in static equilibrium, there should be no net forces or torques and also no acceleration, whether translational or rotational. The best example of static equilibrium is why the leaning tower of Pisa does not fall down. This is because the static force balances it.

FUN FACT

Consider a flowing river. The flow of a river is subject to two forces in equilibrium. The first is the force that accelerates it and the second is the resistance created by the objects in its bed.

Static force balancing the leaning tower of Pisa, Italy.

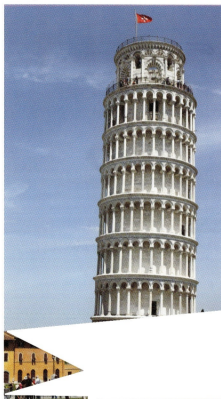

A gymnast suspended in air uses force to hold himself while gravity is acting upon him. His body is in equilibrium.

Elastic Forces

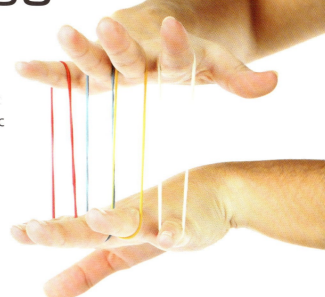

Have you ever thought about why, when we stretch and release it, a rubber band tries to regain its shape? It is because rubber has elastic properties. There is a force that acts on the molecules of a rubber band that resists on being stretched. This force is called an elastic force. It can be defined as a conservative force that arises in an object during its deformation and resists the change in all directions. This force is transmitted through the molecules of the object.

Tension force.

Types of elastic forces

There are two types of elastic forces. One is tension and the other is compression. If any object is stretched, there is a tension force in its molecules and when any object is compressed, there resides the compression force.

A catapult makes use of elastic force to set a body in motion.

Applications

There are many applications of elastic forces. The bow and arrow functions on the basis of elastic force. Elastic property is used in clothing, hair bands, bracelets and for art and craft.

When engineers build huge bridges and flyovers for heavy traffic to pass through, it is not possible for them to create the entire structure out of stone. The foundation is usually industrial quality metal. However, they have to leave gaps in the bridge. This is because they have to consider the temperature. Metal contracts in the cold and expands in the heat. If the foundation of the bridge were to contract and expand, the bridge would crumble away. Hence, gaps are left in the bridge held together with a metal that has a good amount of elasticity. This elasticity allows the metal to expand when heated and contract to its original shape when cooled. Usually, steel is used.

Types of inelastic forces

The types of forces that do not possess elastic property are called inelastic forces; for example, torque, magnetic forces, electrostatic forces or gravitational forces. Inelastic forces are also very important. Inelastic forces are responsible for changing the shape of any object permanently.

How to Measure Forces?

Force, in simple words, is the push or pull of an object. It is measured by many available instruments; whether it is a contact or non-contact force, static or dynamic. By measuring force, we can also measure torque, acceleration, weight and other quantities. Several types of gauges are available for measuring forces.

Apparatus to measure force

Different types of force gauges, spring scales, load cells, mechanical test stands, pneumatic testers, motorised test stands, digital force testers, grips and fixtures, sensors and many accessories are now available in the market for measuring force. The allowable range to measure force using these instruments varies from 103 to 109 newtons. The instruments used are based on the principle that a transducer is made that accepts the force and then changes it into some output, that is, a measurable physical quantity. Instruments from simple technique dial gauge to complex digital converters are now accessible.

A hand compresses the force measurement device, which, in turn, measures the force applied.

Hooke's law apparatus to measure force.

Force measurement devices

A load cell is a common force measuring unit. In general terms, a chain of transducers is called a load cell. Force is calculated by the electrical signal of the magnitude equal to that of the force applied. Hydraulic load cells, pneumatic load cells and strain gauge load cells are some types of load cells. The spring balance is another force-measuring device that is frequently used for various applications. A spring balance is an instrument with a spring and a hook on it that measures the weight of an object very accurately by opposing the gravitational force. It works on the basis of Hooke's law and measures weights from a few newtons to thousands of newtons. Mainly, it is used in industries for measuring heavy loads and as accelerometers.

GRAVITY

Do you know why we can stand on Earth and why everything flies in space? This is caused by a force that attracts two things towards each other, called gravity. Our Earth has a gravitational force. That is why if we jump we are drawn back to Earth. However, in space, there is no gravity which is why astronauts can float about.

It is gravity that causes objects to have weight. When some object has weight, it means that there is a certain amount of gravity acting on that object. The Sun's gravitational pull influences our planet to orbit around it. The motion of the moon is influenced by gravity between the Sun and Earth. The moon's gravity pulls on Earth and makes the tides rise and fall every day. As the moon passes over the ocean, the sea level swells. As Earth rotates, the moon passes over new parts of Earth, causing the oceanic swells to move along with it.

What is Gravitational Force?

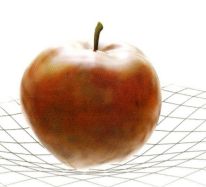

Gravitation is the force of attraction that acts to draw any body together while gravity is the force in operation between Earth and other bodies. Gravity depends on the gravitational field of Earth, as well as on other factors, such as Earth's rotation. The measure of force of gravity for any given body is the weight of that body; however, the mass of any body does not vary with its location. It is the weight that varies.

Gravitational force working on a heavy object.

Gravitational force

Did you know that the same person would weigh slightly different if weighed at different parts of the world? At a given location, objects are equally accelerated by the force of gravity. This is because Earth's rotation can spin any object into space. The gravity of Earth at the equator is 9.789 m/s^2 while the force of gravity at the poles is 9.832 m/s^2. Thus, an object will weigh more at the poles than at the equator because of this centripetal force. This means that weight is a relatively variable number.

Difference in force of gravity

The force of gravity changes depending on what lies beneath any object. Any higher concentrations of mass like high-density rocks can alter the force of gravity on an object slightly.

Calculating gravitational force on Earth

To do this, we need one more factor, a gravitational constant with the value 6.673×10^{-11} Nm^2/kg^2. The force of gravity in our daily life is termed as "weight". Our weight is a measurement of the force of Earth's gravity acting upon us.

Objects falling to Earth due to its gravity.

Acceleration Due to Gravity

We have already learnt in the previous section that any free-falling object is under the influence of gravity. A free-falling object has an acceleration of roughly 9.8 m/s² towards Earth. The numerical value for this acceleration is an important value and has been referred to as the acceleration of gravity, which is the acceleration of objects moving only under the influence of gravity.

Acceleration due to gravity value

Acceleration due to gravity is the numerical value for the acceleration of a free-falling object. It is denoted by the symbol "g". The numerical value for the acceleration of gravity is 9.8 m/s². However, slight variations in this value are primarily influenced by the altitude, increasing or decreasing speed or changing direction of an object. Any free-falling object is always under the influence of gravity with an acceleration of 9.8 m/s² in the downward direction. These free-falling objects are independent from resistance of air. This is gravitational acceleration or acceleration due to gravity, denoted by "g" has a standard value of 9.8 m/s² but varies in gravitational environments. The gravitational field widget is used to investigate the effect of location on the value of "g".

What is acceleration due to gravity?

Among all types of forces, the most common is the force of gravity. It is experienced by us in everyday life. Also, it is present on a global scale. The reason behind objects falling on the ground is the inherent property of Earth exerting a force of attraction on objects. This force is the force of gravity and the acceleration generated on these objects because of this force is acceleration due to gravity. According to the definition of force, the equation of force due to gravity has been denoted by,

$$W = mg$$

where m = the mass of the object and g = acceleration due to gravity.

In this case, force is better known as the weight of objects. Acceleration, in this case, is acceleration due to gravity, which is constant and denoted by g. The approximate value of acceleration due to gravity is 32 ft/s² , or 9.8 m/s². These are the values of acceleration of gravity on Earth.

Application

Hence, if we want to calculate the force (weight) of a ball falling from the top of a building, we would find out its mass in grams and simply multiply this number with 9.8 m/s². This helps to solve a lot of physics-related problems.

Ball falling down due to gravitational force.

Gravity on Moon

Gravity is the force between two objects and not simply the force between an object and Earth. It is the force between the Sun and Earth, moon and Earth and is present anywhere in the universe. The centre of our solar system, the Sun, also has gravity, because of which all the planets revolve around it.

Weight on Earth v/s moon

If we measure our weight on Earth, it can be calculated as the product of the mass of the object and the gravity of Earth, which has a fixed value of 9.8 m/s^2. If we try to measure our weight on the moon, will it be same? The answer is no, as it will depend on the gravity of the moon, which is not the same as that of Earth. The moon is 1/4th the size of Earth; thus, the moon's gravity is much less as compared to Earth's gravity. To be precise, it is 83.3 per cent less. And so, we can assume that if we were to weigh ourself on the moon, our weight would show up to be much less compared to that on Earth. Since the moon's gravitational attraction is less, we can even jump twice the height and distance as compared to that on Earth.

Differences in gravity

In a spaceship, your weight would read zero; you are weightless. If you were on any other celestial body, you would weigh a different amount than you do on Earth. The weight that you feel depends on many things, including your actual mass, the mass of the planet that you are on and how further away you are from the centre of that planet.

FUN FACT

We say that Earth's gravity is weak. But how is that possible when it holds all of us on Earth? Consider a little magnet that sticks to your refrigerator. It just takes that little magnet's electromagnetic force to cancel out the gravitational force acting on it to remain on the refrigerator.

Astronauts spacewalking, as no gravitational force is working on them.

Without gravity, the body feels weightless.

METALS AND
NON-METALS

Metals are a class of substances (they can be a pure element, an alloy or a compound) that are characterised by their high conductivity to heat and electricity, their high malleability, ductility, hardness and reflectivity of light. They have crystalline molecular structures. About 91 of the known elements on the periodic table are metals, and are arranged on the left side and the centre of it.

Non-metals share none of the distinctive characteristics of metals. They are poor conductors of heat and electricity, and are amorphous, non-malleable and highly volatile. There are 17 elements on the periodic table that are classified as non-metals and they are found on the right-hand side of the table.

Alloy

An alloy is the combination of two or more metals or a metal and a non-metal. Alloys, such as brass (copper and zinc) and bronze (copper and tin) were known since the ancient ages. Once an alloy has been formed, it cannot be separated by physical means. Over 90 per cent of the metals we use are alloys.

Making of alloys

Cutting process of hard alloys.

The properties of alloys are quite distinct from their constituents. For example, although aluminium and copper are both very soft and ductile, the resulting aluminium–copper alloy is much harder and stronger. Similarly, the addition of a small amount of non-metal, "carbon" to iron yields an alloy called steel, which is much harder and tougher. Any alloy consists of two constituents, the matrix (primary element) and the alloying elements (the additional element needed to make the alloy). Alloys are generally produced by co-melting the mixture of ingredients. The alternate route for producing alloys is the powder metallurgical route. Alloys are designed with respect to the selection of alloying elements. Their composition is a very difficult and challenging task. Different alloying elements are added to impart specific properties.

Ferrous and non-ferrous alloys

On the basis of commercial importance, alloys can be classified into two groups, ferrous alloys (the primary element is iron) and non-ferrous alloys (the primary element is not iron). Among ferrous alloys, the most important ones are steels. The main alloying elements of steel are Cr, Ni, Mn, Mo, Si, W, V, etc. Steels exhibit a wide range of desirable properties, including hardness, toughness, ductility and corrosion resistance. Copper-nickel, copper-zinc, aluminium alloys, magnesium alloys and nickel alloys are examples of non-ferrous alloys, which are widely used for various engineering components. On the basis of the atomic position of the alloying element, the alloy may be categorised into two groups – atom exchange (substitutional alloy) and interstitial alloy. The relative size of the constituent element of the alloy plays the main role in determining the type of alloy. When the constituent atoms are similar in size, usually, the substitution mechanism takes place, whereas if a wide difference in size exists, interstitial mechanism takes place to form the alloy. Classic examples of substitution alloys are bronze and brass, where some of the Cu atoms are substituted with either Sn or Zn atoms. Fe–C alloy steel is an appropriate example of interstitial alloys.

Alloy wheel caps are used in a car.

Iron

Iron, which has the symbol Fe for its Latin name Ferrum, is one of the oldest elements known to man. Iron is highly valued for its strength and its ability to provide much stronger alloys, such as steel. Iron has hugely contributed to the evolution of the civilisation and shaped it into its current form. Iron is the 26th element on the periodic table.

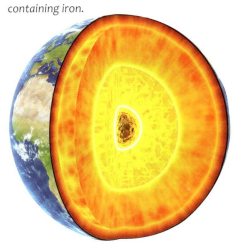

The core of Earth containing iron.

Pyrrhotite is a rare iron sulphide.

Iron in nature

It is the most common element on Earth. It is also common in other planets that have a rocky surface. Earth's inner and outer core is made out of molten iron. Other than iron, even nickel is present in Earth's core. In nature, iron is found to be combined with oxygen molecules to form oxides of iron. These are the most common substances found in Earth's crust. Iron combines with oxygen in different ratios to give different oxides – hematite, magnetite and wustite. Iron oxides are found in abundance in meteorites too.

Reactivity

Iron forms compounds by sharing a multiple number of electrons. Those with a valence of two are called ferrous and those with three are called ferric. Likewise, we have ferrous and ferric oxides. Iron reacts with halogens like chlorine, fluorine or bromine to create halide salts. At high temperatures, iron reacts with sulphur to form iron sulphide, which is commonly known as pyrite or fool's gold.

Steel

Iron is the most common element in Earth's crust. It is vastly used in manufacturing and industries. However, iron is not directly used because of its many drawbacks. It is a relatively soft metal. Also, pure iron combines with atmospheric oxygen in the presence of humidity to form oxides of iron or rust, which makes it weaker. The solution is steel. Steel is an alloy of iron that contains around one per cent carbon. Sometimes, a little manganese is also added. Based on the percentage of carbon and manganese, we get different types of steel that we see around us every day.

Carbon steel is the most widely used version of steel containing one per cent carbon. Stainless steel, contains 12–30 per cent chromium. It also contains traces of nickel.

FUN FACT

Stainless steel is so versatile that it's not only used in making household utensils, ornamental mirrors, photo frames, and imitation jewellery but also in the construction of bridges, buildings and skyscrapers.

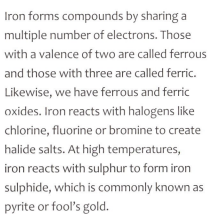

Stainless steel kitchenware.

Superalloys

Superalloys are high-performance alloys that are utilised in extreme situations. These alloys have brilliant mechanical strength; they do not distort under pressure or influence of extreme temperatures and are corrosion, rust or oxidation resistant.

Jet plane engine.

Uses of superalloys

High-performance alloys are primarily utilised in engines that are used in the aerospace and marine industry. Some examples of high-performance alloys or superalloys are Inconel, Hestelloy, TMS alloy, MP98T, RB199 and CMSX single crystal alloys. Superalloys are heavily dependent upon chemical and process inventions. New superalloys are being devised occasionally and have various applications. Nickel-based and cobalt-based superalloys are mostly in demand because of the various advantages they offer.

Elements used

The elements utilised in superalloys have high melting points because the resulting alloy must withstand high temperatures. Nickel is commonly used as the base for such alloys. We also have carbon, tungsten, vanadium, molybdenum, chromium, hafnium, boron and even more elements that are incorporated in these alloys. These alloys experience multi-phase coating. Pack cementation process is a stage conducted at lower temperatures, where the coating material is diffused inwards through the surface. The gas phase coating occurs at thousands of degrees centigrade. Then, the bond coating is performed, which is an adhesive form of coating.

Extreme use

A superalloy is also known as a high-performing alloy. The arms and weapons manufacturers of many countries use this material to create weapons that are easier to carry by soldiers and can withstand the elements of nature at the same time. Scientists are always in the process of developing superalloys that are cheaper to create and lighter in weight, and yet strong enough to survive extreme conditions.

A yacht makes use of superalloys so that it can float as well as avoid rust.

Silicon

Silicon is the second most abundant element in Earth's crust. Earth's crust is made of 28 per cent silicon. It is also the most abundantly found element in the universe. Planetoids and comets, even dust and sand, contain silicon. However, silicon is not present in a free state in nature. Sand is an oxide of silicon. Silicon is a metalloid. It is also a semiconductor and can act as a conductor or a resistor. By nature, silicon is inert but can react with halogens and dilute alkalis.

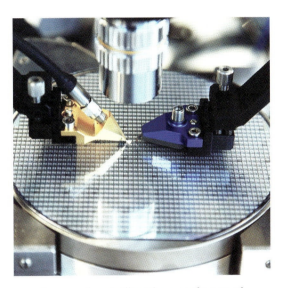

Process of controlling the manufacture of microcircuits on a wafer of silicon.

Glass

Silicon is a major component of glass. If you pick up a handful of sand, half of it is made up of silicon. It is said that glass was invented when ancient Egyptians had studied the effects of lightning striking the sand. Of course, it took many years of experimenting before we arrived at the glass that we use today.

Silicon sand, also known as quartz sand, is melted with carbon up to 2205° C to create glass. As the glass forms, the by-products get released in the form of carbon monoxide gas.

In today's day and age, glass is not only an intricate part of modern architecture; most scientific apparatus are also made of it. We also use it in our daily life for drinking, eating and cooking.

Solar cells made of silicon.

Use in electronics

Silicon has a huge contribution to this era of information. Every single electronic and logic device, even a pocket calculator relies on silicon for functionality. It is extensively used to make transistors, which are electronic switches. These switches can collectively build logic gates. These logic gates successively form complicated microprocessors, microcontrollers and flash memory, all of which are essential in today's world. The silicon used to make electronic devices are known as electronic grade silicon. Electronic grade silicon is very pure; more than 99.9 per cent pure. Silicon is also used to make solar cells.

Light Alloys

Light alloys are based on aluminium, titanium, beryllium and magnesium. These alloys are light, but they also have great mechanical strength. This means that they have a good strength to density ratio. They are commonly used in building vehicles like cars, rockets and aeroplanes. They are also used in the shipbuilding industry. The commonly used alloys in the construction industry are iron and nickel based.

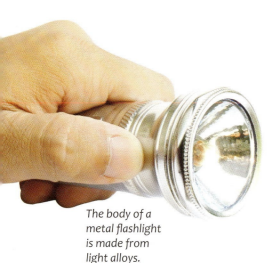

The body of a metal flashlight is made from light alloys.

Electronics are also made from light alloys.

Electronics

Usually, magnesium alloys are used to make chassis for electronic goods. Expensive professional cameras use magnesium alloy chassis to withstand rough usage. For such alloys, magnesium is mixed with lithium and a few other elements. Other expensive electronics like flagship tablets and smartphones also have metallic bodies that are crafted from aluminium or magnesium alloys. These make the devices lighter and portable. Also, because of their high tensile strength, they are resistant to drops and bumps. In larger scales, light alloys are used extensively in automotive engineering. Making cars lighter gives them more mileage. They are also used in nuclear power engineering and civil engineering.

Aviation

Aluminium alloys are majorly used in the construction of aeroplanes. This is because this alloy is light, economical and a bad conductor of electricity. Due to this, it does not put a lot of pressure on the engines while flying, subsequently consuming less fuel. Since the material is cheap, it tends to be economically feasible. Also, there is very less chance of the plane being hit by lightning when in flight due to the non-conducing properties of the alloy. There are other materials that are being developed to replace aluminium in the aviation industry; however, they still have to prove their reliability.

Other applications

Other than electronics and aviation, light alloys are also used in many other items of our daily use. Some household utensils, mostly the ones that are large in size, are made of light alloys. They are also used in the manufacturing of bicycle parts, as it makes it easier for the rider. Daily items like soda cans and metal flashlights are also made from these. Also, a lot of costume jewellery makes use of light alloys. As this type of jewellery is usually elaborate, the light alloys ensure that not only do they look ornamental but also don't cause undue discomfort to the wearer.

A soda can made from a light alloy.

ELECTRICITY

Electricity is the set of physical occurrences related to the flow and presence of electrical charge. There are a wide variety of events associated with electricity, namely, electrical current, static electricity, lightning and electromagnetic induction. The creation of electromagnetic radiation was possible due to electricity. It produces charges which in turn produce electromagnetic fields, which act on other charges. The word "electricity" comes from the Greek word "ilektrismós" meaning amber. In traditional times, amber was rubbed together to produce electrical charges or effects. However, it is only during the second half of the nineteenth century, that its practical applications came into being.

Electricity Production

Think of your life from the time you wake up to the time you go to bed. In this modern world, we are totally dependent upon electricity from charging our mobile to entertaining ourselves with television or music systems, from adding with hot water to preparation of food items in the microwave. We use electricity everywhere.

A cellphone being charged.

Electricity production

Generation of electricity is the conversion of any one form of energy into electricity. It is not exactly the generation of energy. As the law of conservation states, energy can neither be created nor destroyed. This initial energy that is converted into electricity is often called primary energy as this sort of energy is readily available in nature. A prime example of such energy is wind energy or solar energy. These two examples are also clean energy sources as the process of converting them to electricity does not harm the environment.

A man starting a generator.

In general, the term "generation of electricity" is mostly concerned with the entire process of converting one form of energy to electricity, taking it from where it is usable to an entire city and then distributing it to various homes.

Basic principle of electricity production

The basic principle that is used in these systems that help generate electricity was proposed by Michael Faraday. He stated that electricity is generated in a loop of wire when it is moved between the poles of a magnet. A more formal Faraday's Law was formulated from it too. Before transmission and distribution of electricity, the fundamental generation of electricity uses the discovery of Faraday in 1830s, that is, conversion of movement or mechanical energy into electricity. The process includes turbines that are rotated using various sources of energy like wind, water, gas and steam. It lights a spark that gets collected by a generator and distributed elsewhere as usable electricity.

Solar and photovoltaic energy

Solar and photovoltaic cells are the best renewable source of energy. They convert solar energy to electrical energy using semiconductors. These cells turn energy from the Sun's rays directly into instantly usable energy. There are two main types: solar thermal and photovoltaic. Solar thermal panels utilise the Sun's energy to heat water that can be used in washing and heating. Photovoltaic panels utilise the photovoltaic effect to turn the Sun's energy directly into electricity.

Solar panels convert solar energy to electricity.

Fuel combustion

Traditional materials like coal and natural gas are used as fuel in many power stations. These are used to heat water and generate steam, which rotates the turbine and generates electricity. Coal is the major source of fuel for electricity generation. Most power stations require huge reserves of coal to produce electricity continuously. However, coal combustion not only leaves by-products but is also replenishable. Hence, alternative, efficient resources are being looked into.

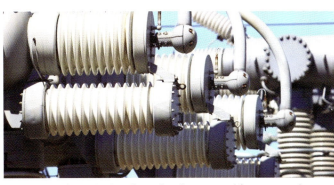

Electricity is collected and generated from power houses.

Hydroelectricity

Hydroelectricity generation is the method used to generate electricity by harnessing the power of moving water, known as hydroelectric power. To produce electricity from the kinetic energy in moving water, the water has to move with adequate speed and volume to spin a propeller-like device called a turbine, which in turn rotates a generator. For instance, about four litres of water per second falling one hundred feet can generate one kilowatt of electricity.

Dams are used to harness water and create electricity.

Wind power

Wind power is a great source of electricity generation, currently. In the areas near the sea coast and vast deserts, this method has got great success. A wind turbine works on the principle of using wind harnessed mechanical energy to make electricity. Wind turns the blades of the windmills, which spin a shaft, which is connected to a generator that generates electricity. These turbines convert kinetic energy in the wind into mechanical energy. Wind turbines can be built on land or offshore in large bodies of water such as oceans and lakes.

Windmills are used to generate electricity.

Electromagnetism

Electromagnetism is the study of the electromagnetic force. It is a type of physical interaction that occurs between electrically charged particles. It is one of the four fundamental interactions that exist in nature, others being strong interaction, weak interaction and gravitation. It is the force exerted by the electromagnetic interaction of electrically charged or magnetically polarised particles or bodies.

What is electromagnetism?

One of the four fundamental forces, electromagnetic force manifests itself through forces between the charges (Coulomb's Law) and magnetic force. These forces are together described through the Lorentz force law. Theoretically, both magnetic and electric forces are manifestations of an exchange force involving the exchange of photons. Electromagnetic force is a force of infinite range, which obeys the conventional inverse square law.

A Magnetic Resonance Imaging (MRI) machine makes use of electromagnetism.

Where does it act?

Electromagnetism manifests as both electric fields and magnetic fields. Both fields are simply different aspects of electromagnetism and, hence, are intrinsically related. Thus, a changing electric field generates a magnetic field; conversely, a changing magnetic field generates an electric field. This effect is known as the electromagnetic induction.

Teacher conducting an experiment on electromagnetism.

FUN FACT

A common misconception about electricity was that it was discovered by Benjamin Franklin. While he did prove the existence and science of electricity using the kite experiment, humans have known about electricity since the times of the Ancient Greeks.

Applications

The principle of electromagnetism is the basis of the operation of electrical generators, motors and transformers. The magnetic and electric fields are convertible with relative motion as four vectors. In quantum electrodynamics, electromagnetic interactions between charged particles can be calculated using the method of Feynman diagrams. It is used in scrap metal yards to pick up heavy loads of metal and in MRI machines in hospitals.